Billie Holiday

MAGDALENA ALAGNA

the rosen publishing group's
rosen
central

Published in 2003 by The Rosen Publishing Group, Inc.
29 East 21st Street, New York, NY 10010

First Edition

Library of Congress Cataloging-in-Publication Data

Alagna, Magdalena.
Billie Holiday / by Magdalena Alagna.—1st ed.
p. cm. — (Rock & roll hall of famers)
Includes discography (p.), bibliographical references (p.), and index.
ISBN 0-8239-3640-6 (library binding)
1. Holiday, Billie, 1915-1959–Juvenile literature. 2. Singers—United States—Biography—Juvenile literature. I. Title. II. Series.
ML3930.H64 A78 2003
782.42165'092—dc21

2002004540

Manufactured in the United States of America

CONTENTS

Introduction 5

1. God Bless the Child 12

2. Harlem 26

3. Smooth Sailing in the Swing Era 40

4. Celebrated and Disgraced 56

5. The Late 1940s and Early 1950s 72

6. The End, the Legacy 90

Selected Discography 102

Glossary 103

To Find Out More 105

For Further Reading 107

Index 109

Billie Holiday is widely considered to be one of the greatest singers of the twentieth century.

Introduction

Billie Holiday was one of the most influential jazz singers ever to grace the music scene. Ralph Gleason, in his book *Celebrating the Duke*, wrote: "She was a singer of jazz, the greatest female jazz voice of all time, a great interpreter, a great actress and the creator of a style that, in its own way, is as unique and important to jazz as the styles

of Louis Armstrong, Charlie Parker and Lester Young. She did something no other woman has ever done in jazz. Today, if you sing jazz and you're a woman, you sing some of Billie Holiday."

Billie Holiday was born into poverty, was raised by a single mother, and lived through the Great Depression. Billie did odd jobs around the neighborhood, eventually working in a brothel. This was the first place she heard blues and jazz music, such as the recordings of Bessie Smith and Louis Armstrong, which would be so influential in developing her own musical style. Listening to the music she loved was the way she escaped her troubles.

The tragic events of her life are part of the legend of Billie Holiday. Some say that it was her knowledge of hardship that gave her the painful experience to sing with such emotion. Holiday herself said, "What comes out is what I feel. I hate straight singing. I have to change a tune to my own way of doing it. That's all I know." Others point out that her father, Clarence Holiday, was a musician with one of the best orchestras in the early jazz music scene and that

Billie Holiday's music talent may, in part, have been inherited.

It could be said that Billie Holiday was unimaginably brave in the way that only artists are. She created and reinvented herself through her wide range of singing styles. She could sing light, airy melodies as well as "torch" songs, the slow and sentimental songs for which she became popular. She changed forever the way people thought about music. When you consider her contributions to jazz and her extraordinary talent, you see a beautiful, magical side of Billie Holiday. Billie practiced her art in the face of racism so extreme that her tours through many parts of America became nightmares during which, at times, she could not find places to eat, go to the bathroom, or sleep. This is because much of the country was still segregated during the 1930s. Segregation ensured that black people and white people were kept separated as much as possible. The facilities for blacks were supposed to be equal to those provided for whites, but that was seldom the case. Blacks often had to contend with inferior facilities.

It is important to remember the many different parts of Billie Holiday's life, career, and personality. She was an extremely complex person. She was a pioneering artist. Among her many achievements, Billie Holiday popularized the song "Strange Fruit," which she recorded in 1939. It was a song about a lynching that took place in a southern town. The song helped to shed some light on the treatment of blacks in America and to pave the way for civil rights awareness. It took a lot of courage to sing such a song in the 1930s, when there was still so much racism in America.

Billie Holiday's work with the Benny Goodman Orchestra and the Artie Shaw Orchestra is among some of her most memorable music. Her work with Benny Goodman is also notable because Goodman was among the first white band leaders to include a black woman in his band. Holiday also wrote some of the songs that she sang. One of the most famous is "God Bless the Child." Not surprisingly, Holiday wrote a song based on her own experiences. "God Bless the Child" is about a

Billie Holiday, with her band, including the piano player James P. Johnson, performs the song "Fine and Mellow."

child's ability to fend for himself in a hard world: "God bless the child that's got his own."

She played some of the biggest concert halls of the day, including Carnegie Hall, performed at the Metropolitan Opera House in New York City, and wowed the notoriously tough-to-please crowd at the Apollo Theater. She contributed significantly to the success of Cafe Society, New York City's first racially integrated nightclub, in Greenwich Village.

Billie Holiday's peak is generally thought to be during the 1930s, which was the heyday of swing music, also called big band music. Her early years of singing were in Harlem during Prohibition, when selling alcohol was illegal. This means that much of her early performing was done in speakeasies, or places that sold illegal alcohol. Prohibition was repealed in 1933, and many of the speakeasies became nightclubs. It was in Monette's, a popular nightclub, that she astonished a young John Hammond. John was fresh out of college and starting his career as a music critic and record producer. John said of the first time he heard Billie: "To my astonishment, she sang a completely different chorus to the same tune at each table. It was the first really improvising singer that I heard."

Although many jazz critics believe that Holiday's art had declined by the 1950s, her voice roughened by alcohol and drugs, there are just as many people who disagree. Some feel that the later Billie Holiday recordings, such as the album *Lady in Satin*, recorded in 1958 and one of her best-selling albums, are perfect examples of her unmatched ability to convey emotion through song.

There are many sides to Billie Holiday. You can choose to remember her as a passionate, beautiful, troubled woman, or as an inventive and courageous artist. She rose above the unfortunate circumstances of her childhood, yet allowed herself to be destroyed by addiction. Read on to learn more about this complex woman.

1 God Bless the Child

It is difficult at times to pin down the truth about the events of Billie Holiday's life. This is in part because Holiday herself invented and reinvented certain details of her life in interviews and in her autobiography, *Lady Sings the Blues*, ghostwritten by her journalist friend William Dufty. Many of the biographies that have been written about Billie

Holiday have even gotten her birthplace wrong! For a long time, it was thought that she was born in Baltimore, Maryland, which is where her mother lived and where Billie grew up. However, Billie (born Eleanora Fagan) was born on April 7, 1915, in Philadelphia, Pennsylvania. Sadie Fagan, her mother, was thirteen years old when she was born. Clarence Holiday, her father, was fifteen years old.

Billie Holiday's Parents

Sadie Fagan wanted her daughter to be born in Philadelphia because hospital deliveries were performed there, unlike in Baltimore, where babies were usually delivered by midwives, at home. Eleanora's father, Clarence Holiday, never married Sadie Fagan. This is another fact of Billie Holiday's life that remained a secret for a long time. Holiday said in her autobiography that her parents got married when she was three years old and that they were married for a short time but were eventually divorced. But other sources say that Sadie and Clarence were never married at all.

Clarence Holiday was a neglectful father. He had served in the United States Army during World War I, and from the 1920s onward, he was a jazz guitar player with Fletcher Henderson's orchestra. Fletcher Henderson's band was one of the best and most popular of the early big bands. Clarence spent much of his time traveling. He did get married to a woman in New York, but it is uncertain whether Sadie knew about this. When Clarence was in Baltimore, he would visit Sadie and Eleanora. He entranced his young daughter with stories about playing music in Henderson's band. One of his nicknames for his daughter was Bill because she was such a tough little tomboy. It was this fact, together with Eleanora's admiration for film star Billie Dove, that led her to later change her name to Billie.

Relations between Billie and her father became a little strained when she moved to New York City and began to have some success in music. Clarence told her not to tell people that she was his daughter. He didn't want anyone to think that he was old enough to have a daughter as old as Billie was. He told John Hammond,

Billie's record producer, that she was "something I stole when I was fifteen." It is perhaps not surprising that Billie Holiday's father did finally acknowledge her when she started to gain success as a singer. He complained at times that his daughter did not use his services as a guitarist as much as she could have on her recordings and tours. It seems sure that this was intentional on Billie's part and that she was taking revenge on her father for his neglect by not giving him work.

As a girl, Billie admired her father. She identified much more with her father's glamorous lifestyle of being a traveling musician than she did with her mother's lifestyle. Sadie Fagan worked as a maid. She worked long, hard hours for very little pay. "I ain't gonna be no maid," Billie Holiday often said throughout her life. It was hard for Billie to understand why she should follow the rules, work hard, and go to school as her mother told her to do. All that Billie saw was her mother's hard work, which resulted in poverty. On the other hand, Clarence Holiday was living a fabulous life and making far more money playing music in illegal speakeasies until all hours of the night.

Early Family Experiences

Many of Sadie's family members looked down on her for being an unwed mother. With Clarence gone and work in Baltimore difficult to find, Sadie often left Billie in the care of relatives. Although her grandfather and great-grandmother were kind to her, Billie included many stories in her autobiography about the cruel treatment she received from her cousin Ida. Billie said Cousin Ida beat her.

Sadie's father cared about Sadie and Billie, and tried to help them out with money. His mother, Billie's great-grandmother, was, according to Billie, also a beloved early influence in the girl's life. However, there is some evidence to suggest that this was another of Holiday's inventions and that she may not have known her great-grandmother at all. According to *Lady Sings the Blues,* this great-grandmother had been a slave in Virginia. She had given birth to seventeen children fathered by the white, Irish plantation owner who owned her. "We used to talk about life," Billie remembered in *Lady Sings the Blues*, "and she used to tell me how it felt to be a slave, to be owned body and soul. She couldn't read or write, but she knew the Bible, and she was always ready to tell me a story from the Scriptures."

One of the bizarre events of Billie Holiday's early life has to do with her great-grandmother. It should be mentioned that, although Billie described this event in shocking detail in her autobiography, there is some doubt about whether the story is true. As the story goes, one night, the old woman persuaded the girl to let her sleep lying down. She normally slept sitting up because of a lung ailment that made it dangerous for her to lie on her back, but Billie didn't know that. She helped her great-grandmother to lie down, and she lay down beside her. She woke up hours later with the old woman's rigid arm around her neck. The great-grandmother had died in her sleep. It took a month's stay in the hospital until Billie could recover from the shock. When she went home, Cousin Ida beat her for causing the old woman's death.

Sadie often left Billie to the care of relatives in Baltimore while she worked in New York City and tried to save enough money to have her daughter come and live with her. Billie grew up feeling lonely and unloved. People have come to dwell on this fact of Billie Holiday's upbringing, saying that it was this loneliness and feelings of rejection from her parents that led to her substance abuse later in life. However, there have been many performers raised by relatives, among them

Did You Know?

Although Billie Holiday was not a blues singer, she did record some blues tunes. In the 1940s, she recorded six songs that blues singer Bessie Smith had also recorded, among them "St. Louis Blues" and "Gimme a Pigfoot."

Ella Fitzgerald and Louis Armstrong, who went on to have stable and successful lives. It is clear that we cannot blame all of Billie's problems on her upbringing.

Discovering Jazz Music

Billie escaped the oppressive atmosphere of her house by going to work. She did the cleaning for several houses and ran errands for Alice Dean. Alice Dean's house was a house of prostitution with a record player in the front room. Many times Billie took her pay in the form of being allowed to listen to recordings by Bessie Smith and Louis Armstrong again and again. This was her first exposure to jazz music, and it had a profound influence on her later musical style.

Sadie worried about her daughter being exposed to the influences in Alice Dean's house. Billie didn't care that Alice Dean's was a house of prostitution. Billie had interest only in the music. She said, "If I'd heard Louis and Bessie at a Girl Scout jamboree, I'd have loved it just the same. If I'd heard Pops and Bessie wailing through the window of some minister's front parlor, I'd have been running free errands for him."

Billie had a comparatively limited vocal range, and her voice was not a big, belting voice like Bessie Smith's. Also, she was not a horn player as Louis Armstrong was. Still, she said, "I got my manner from Bessie Smith and Louis Armstrong, honey. I wanted [Bessie's] feeling and Louis' style." She was attracted to Louis Armstrong's sound in particular, and she tried to copy vocally what he did with his horn. "I don't think I'm singing. I feel like I'm playing a horn. I try to improvise like Les Young or Louis Armstrong or someone else I admire," she said later of her singing.

Sent Away

For a while things seemed to be going well for Billie. Sadie moved back to Baltimore and got married to Phil Gough, who treated both Sadie and her daughter very well. However, he died shortly after the marriage. Billie was dealt another crushing blow when she was just ten

The legendary trumpeter Louis Armstrong *(left)* was a major influence on Billie Holiday.

years old: She was raped by a neighbor and accused of "seducing" the man who had raped her. She was forced to go to a Catholic reformatory for her misbehavior. Billie often skipped school to hang around in Alice Dean's front parlor, listening to records, so she may have been sent away regardless of the rape. Either way, she was forced to go to the reformatory.

Billie hated life at the reform home. She had nightmares about it even in her adult life. "For years I used to dream about it and wake up hollering and screaming," Billie wrote in her autobiography. "My God, it's terrible what something like this does to you. It takes years and years to get over it; it haunts you and haunts you." In a gruesome echo of what had happened to Billie with her great-grandmother's death, one of the ways in which the girl was punished at the home was to be locked in a room with the corpse of a classmate. She screamed and pounded on the door until her hands were bloody. It was this experience that led Sadie to petition the court for Billie's release.

Sadie tried to keep her daughter with her as much as possible. Billie's time was divided during the next few years between Baltimore and New York City. She continued to work hard to earn money, scrubbing floors after school. In 1928, after a failed attempt to get Billie to hold down a job as a maid in a home in Long Branch, New Jersey, Sadie sent Billie to live in Harlem. Sadie thought that Billie was renting a room in a boarding house, a place where people can rent private rooms and usually take meals together in a common room. But what Sadie didn't know was that Billie was living in a house of prostitution in Harlem, and she soon became a call girl.

1915
On April 7, Billie Holiday (originally Eleanora Fagan) is born in Philadelphia, Pennsylvania.

1928
Billie moves to Harlem, in New York City.

1932
Billie is hired by Jerry Preston to work nights singing at the Log Cabin.

1935
Billie wows the crowd during her first performance at the Apollo Theater in New York City.

1937
Billie is hired to sing regularly with the Count Basie Orchestra. She is paid $14 a day—more than if she were performing in clubs.

1938
The Artie Shaw Orchestra hires Billie to sing. It is one of the first times that a black woman is hired to sing with a white band.

1943
Esquire magazine names Billie Holiday the best jazz vocalist in a critics poll.

1944
Decca Records gives Billie a contract. She is allowed to record with a string section—an unusual honor at that time.

1947
In May, Billie is arrested for possession of narcotics. She spends nine and a half months in jail.

1954
Billie travels to Europe for her first European tour. She performs in Scandinavia, Germany, Holland, Belgium, France, Switzerland, and England.

1956
William Dufty, a writer for the *New York Post*, begins ghostwriting *Lady Sings the Blues*, the autobiography of Billie Holiday.

1959
Frankie Freedom, a well-known jazz singer, finds Billie collapsed on the floor of her apartment. Against her wishes, she is taken to the hospital, where she passes away after forty-four days.

2

Harlem

Harlem was a terrific place to be in 1928. It was a lively center for black arts and culture. The explosion of artistry that had taken place in Harlem was called the Harlem Renaissance. The Harlem Renaissance of the 1920s and 1930s was mainly a black literary movement. Some people do not consider visual art or music part of the Harlem Renaissance, but others do. The Harlem Renaissance

may have started under the influence of W. E. B. DuBois, the editor of *The Crisis* from 1910 to 1934. DuBois was outspoken about the need for blacks to celebrate their unique African American culture and heritage. The works of prominent authors Zora Neale Hurston and Langston Hughes also helped to set the tone of the Harlem Renaissance, which was about black self-expression, empowerment, identity, and creativity.

Prohibition

The Harlem Renaissance was not the only unique feature in New York City at this time. Prohibition was the period in America from 1920 to 1933 during which it was illegal to make, buy, sell, or drink alcohol. Of course, many people never let Prohibition stop them from doing what they wanted to do. They just had to carry on underground, away from the eyes of the law. Some people made alcohol in their homes and sold it. They were called bootleggers. Some people operated places where the bootleggers could bring their alcohol and where people could gather to drink, listen to music, and have a good time. These places were called speakeasies. They were run in secret, often in basements and other out-of-the-way places.

At the time Billie Holiday arrived in Harlem, there was a lot going on. It was the place to be for anyone who knew anything about music and culture. Many people, both blacks and whites, made the trip uptown when they wanted to experience something new and exceptional. There was plenty for a young girl in Harlem to do to have a good time.

Billie Holiday arrived in Harlem in 1928. She was thirteen, and she was living in a house of prostitution. She quickly became a $20 call girl. She used the money she earned to buy herself nice clothes, such as silk dresses, stockings, and high-heeled shoes. Her career was cut short, however, when she refused to go with a man who was an influential customer. He had her arrested for being a "wayward woman." She would have gone to another reformatory, but Sadie lied for her and told the judge that her daughter was eighteen. She was sentenced to an adult correctional facility.

During the 1920s and 1930s, New York City's Harlem, including this block on Lenox Avenue, was the vital center of African American culture.

According to her autobiography, Holiday spent four months in a women's prison. She spent part of that time in solitary confinement, which means she was locked away all by herself, where she got only bread to eat and water to drink.

When she got out of jail, Holiday moved into an apartment with her mother. This was during the Great Depression, which was a time of economic crisis in America. Many people had trouble finding work. Sadie and Billie worked hard to try to pay the rent.

Sadie got sick, too sick to work. Billie took to visiting her father, who was again in New York City, and asking him to loan her money. He didn't want anyone to hear her calling him "daddy." He was afraid that it would ruin his image as a man-about-town if anyone found out he had a daughter Billie's age.

The Audition at Pod's and Jerry's

Billie Holiday's beginnings in the Harlem music scene has been the stuff of legend. It has been said that she got her first singing job after an audition at the popular club run by Jerry Preston, called Pod and Jerry's Log Cabin or just Pod's and Jerry's.

Biographers of Billie Holiday's life find it highly unlikely that this was the actual start of Holiday's singing career in Harlem. It is likely that she had been singing in clubs for a while but had not gotten any noteworthy steady or regular gigs. But the music culture of the time was so free and easy that musicians and singers could pop into and out of clubs and perform. It was a good way to earn a few dollars a night, but it took a long time and a lot of hard work to turn singing into a regular paying proposition.

The legend has it that Sadie was too sick even to walk and, on the evening before they would be kicked out of their apartment for not making the rent, Billie Holiday was determined to get a job. She combed the streets and went into many nightclubs looking for work. She ended up at the Log Cabin, where she tried to get a job as a dancer. The only problem was that her dancing was terrible. She was such a bad dancer that the piano player felt sorry for her. He asked her if she could sing. She was bewildered. To her, singing was as natural as breathing. It had never occurred to her that she could get a job singing. She asked the pianist to play "Trav'lin All Alone" because "that came closer than anything to the way I felt," she later said. The song speaks of a person traveling all alone, tired and weary.

It was 1932, and Billie was not even seventeen years old yet. Jerry Preston hired Billie Holiday for eighteen dollars a week, and she sang every night from midnight to 3 AM. By 1933, a lot of people had come to hear her at the Log Cabin.

Early Praise

Billie Holiday didn't just sing at the Log Cabin during this time. Jazz was not a formal style of music, one that always stuck to the same singer doing the same songs at the same club. It encouraged improvisation. Many singers and musicians dropped in and out of clubs to perform. John Hammond, who would later become her record producer when she was recording at Columbia Records, heard her at Monette's Club. As he wrote in his column in the April 1933 issue of *Melody Maker*, "This month there has been a real find in the person of a singer named Billie Halliday [sic] . . . although only 18 she weighs over 200 lbs., is incredibly beautiful and sings as well as anybody I ever heard."

For a little while, Sadie ran a restaurant out of their apartment. She was famous for her chicken and for her soft heart. She often gave hungry people food on credit. It has been suggested that it was in part because of Sadie's generosity that the restaurant was never a success. Billie described their home as "a boardin' house for broke musicians, soup kitchen for anyone with a hard-luck story, community center,

Fun Fact!

Billie Holiday has a theater named after her. It's called the Billie Holiday Theatre, and it is located in Brooklyn, New York. It has featured plays starring Samuel L. Jackson and Debbie Allen, among other prominent African American actors.

The influential and talented jazz saxophonist Lester Young was one of the many friends Billie Holiday made as a young singer.

and after-hours joint . . . All you had to do was tell Mom you were a musician and give her a little story and she'd give you everything in the house that wasn't nailed down."

It was a great musical education for Billie to have so many musicians in her home. She got into discussions about music and musical technique with some of the greatest musicians of her day. She made many friends, among them Lester Young, the jazz saxophonist. He was the one who gave her the nickname Lady Day. She, in turn, called him Prez, short for President, "because he was the world's greatest," Billie said. Lester performed with some of the best orchestras of the day, including Fletcher Henderson's and Count Basie's. Lester influenced a whole generation of jazz musicians, such as John Coltrane and Sonny Rollins.

Lester Young was not the only one who called Billie Holiday a lady. People had been calling her that ever since she worked at the Log Cabin. It was the custom in bars at this time for performers to go from table to

Famous bandleader Benny Goodman plays the clarinet in 1945.

table singing. The customers would put the singers' tips on the tables, and the singers would pick up the bills without using their hands. Billie Holiday wouldn't do that, mainly because she was clumsy and couldn't do it correctly. Still, her fellow singers sneered, "Look at her, she thinks she's a lady," whenever Holiday accepted a tip by using her hands.

The Beginning of a Career in Music

It is at this point that Billie Holiday's career was really starting to take off. John Hammond introduced her to Benny Goodman. Shortly afterward, she made her first record. She then worked with some of the greatest orchestras of the day, including Benny Goodman's, Count Basie's, and Artie Shaw's. In the next chapter, you'll find out who these jazz greats were and how they helped Billie Holiday's career. You'll read about how her unusual approach to jazz music and her unique personality combined to create a legendary performer who would change the future of music.

Artie Shaw, here playing the clarinet in the studio, was another famous bandleader that Billie worked with.

How Jazz Is Different from Blues

People often confuse jazz music with blues music, although the two forms are different. Billie Holiday was not a blues singer, but she did sing a few blues songs. She was a jazz singer, and most of her repertoire was jazz songs. Holiday was a unique jazz singer in part because one of her influences was blues singer Bessie Smith. It can be said that Billie was jazz as far as her singing style went but that she was a blues singer when it came to transmitting her feelings through song.

According to *Rolling Stone* magazine, after the Civil War, African rhythms and European music combined to create what eventually became the blues. The field holler used by slaves to communicate with each other in a way that the whites could not immediately understand became the spiritual song that helped to shape the blues. One of the hallmarks of blues music is the lyric content, which is often a graphic description of suffering. The blues traveled north from New Orleans, Louisiana, and got absorbed into the big band repertoires.

Composer and musician Jelly Roll Morton (1885–1941) claimed that he invented jazz as a twelve-year-old boy in New Orleans, combining ragtime, blues, and some of the French folk music popular in New Orleans at that time. Whether or not that is actually the case, you can see from this short description that the two types of music are similar but that they are two distinctly different forms.

3 Smooth Sailing in the Swing Era

Jazz is an entirely American form of music. It is a combination of many different musical forms, including ragtime music, field hollers of the slave tradition, and gospel music. There are different kinds of jazz, too. Louis Armstrong became famous for playing a kind of jazz called Dixieland jazz, the kind of jazz music associated with New Orleans, where Armstrong was from. It is safe to say that Armstrong was the primary person responsible for bringing this form of jazz, as well as the spirit of improvisation and the singing style called scat, to Harlem.

The 1930s are known as the Swing Era. Swing jazz was jazz that was played by a large orchestra and with complicated arrangements rather than the improvisation of Dixieland jazz. Also, swing jazz was more danceable, so it was popular with the crowds who wanted to go out to clubs to dance. Dances such as the jitterbug were important features of the swing culture. Count Basie's and Duke Ellington's bands are the two most important examples of swing bands. Billie Holiday's life and career were influenced by some of the most influential musicians of the 1930s. These were good years for her singing career, as her success was building and she was becoming more and more popular.

Billie and Benny

Benny Goodman grew up in Chicago, Illinois. He was involved with music at a very young age,

joining local and school bands. When he was fourteen, he joined the musician's union and played gigs around Chicago. He also met the famous jazz cornetist Bix Beiderbecke that year and was greatly influenced by Beiderbecke's style. Goodman also soaked up the music of Louis Armstrong and other jazz greats. Benny arrived in New York City in 1928 as a horn player with Ben Pollack's band. From 1929 to 1934, Benny was one of the most sought-after studio musicians of the day. He met John Hammond and jazz pianist Teddy Wilson, with whom Billie Holiday also worked frequently, during this time. In 1934, Benny set up his first big band and started recording with them for Columbia Records.

Benny Goodman met Billie Holiday in 1933. John Hammond was so impressed with Billie that he took Benny to see her perform. Not only was Benny impressed, he was terribly attracted to the beautiful, talented singer. She was attracted to him, too. They dated for a while, although it has been suggested by various biographers that neither of their families was happy with their romance.

Benny led the band that was in the studio for Billie's first commercial record—the first record for which she would be paid. Although she was paid to record the tunes, Billie never got any royalties from any of her wonderful records.

1935: Billie Holiday's High Points

Billie sang at a number of clubs around New York City, such as Monette's, the Alhambra Grill, and the Hot-Cha Bar and Grill, among others. In 1935, she sang at the Apollo Theater, which was (and still is!) a benchmark for success in any performer's career. Frank Cooper, the master of ceremonies at the Apollo Theater, saw Billie in a club one night and recommended her act to the Apollo's owner, who promptly booked her. Frank Cooper liked Billie so much that he helped her to get a nice dress and shoes for her performance. Backstage, waiting to go on at the Apollo, she was so nervous that one of her fellow performers had to shove her onto the stage to help her get over her stage fright. But she was able to completely win the crowd over. This

Music producer and critic John Hammond was a big fan of Billie's and helped her in many ways.

was not an easy feat, considering the notoriously hard-to-please audience at the Apollo.

There are many reasons why 1935 was such a good year for Billie. Prohibition had been repealed, and there was a lot of work for singers in nightclubs. Also, John Hammond got Billie a lot of sessions at the American Record Corporation (ARC). These sessions were intended to produce records for the new jukebox market. Billie was listed as a featured vocalist, with Teddy Wilson leading the studio band. These sessions contain some of her most famous work.

1936: Billie Holiday and Her Orchestra

In 1936, Joe Glaser became Billie's manager. It was under Joe's management that Billie got to fulfill a musician's dream—performing with Fletcher Henderson's orchestra in the Grand Terrace Ballroom in Chicago, Illinois. Unfortunately, the owner of the club was a racist who took an immediate dislike to Billie Holiday. In fact, he told her that her singing stank.

Billie held her temper for as long as she could—for two days. As the story goes, Billie ended up screaming at the owner and throwing an inkwell at his head. She got no support from either Fletcher Henderson or her manager, Joe Glaser, and she returned to New York City broke and disappointed.

Also in 1936, Billie was working at the Uptown House when she met her future husband, Jimmy Monroe. Another important event in 1936 was that

Did You Know?

Sylvia Sims, a jazz singer who worked with Billie at a club called Kelly's Stable, suggested that Holiday wear a gardenia in her hair. Sylvia gave Billie a white gardenia to wear because Billie had burnt her hair with a curling iron one night before a performance, and the gardenia hid the burn. Billie liked the beautiful flower so much that she always wore it onstage after that. It became her trademark.

ARC decided to do more records with Billie Holiday, this time using her name on the record instead of Teddy Wilson's name. These recording sessions were done with a new producer because John Hammond was scouring the country on a search for talent. He rediscovered Count Basie, whom he had seen perform in 1932. This time, Lester Young was with Basie's orchestra.

Billie Holiday's Time with Count Basie

Billie Holiday got fourteen dollars a day to tour with Count Basie's orchestra. Fourteen dollars a day was more than she could make at a club; she had gotten eighteen dollars a week at Pod's and Jerry's. Lester Young would also be going on the tour, and Billie looked forward to seeing the country, playing music, and having a good time. The reality wasn't as much fun as she had anticipated. For one thing, the pay didn't stretch so far when she had to factor in her expenses and the cost of evening gowns and getting her hair done. Also, the band traveled everywhere by bus. Traveling by bus is very grueling and uncomfortable. The orchestra played the South and the Midwest. They played for black audiences and for white audiences. They encountered racism everywhere the tour took them.

Billie said in her autobiography that one of the fun parts of working with Count Basie was the improvisation. Up until she toured with Basie's band, Billie's experience had been mainly as a session musician in the recording studios, where the music was done by a musical arranger. Billie enjoyed the improvisational approach to music in Basie's band, saying, "The cats would come in, somebody would hum a tune. Then someone else would play it over on the piano once or twice. Then someone would set up a riff [rhythmic pattern], a ba-deep, a ba-dop. Then Daddy Basie would two-finger it a little. And then things would start to happen."

Billie was with Count Basie's orchestra for two years. She quit when the band was playing in Detroit, Michigan. A club manager wanted her to blacken her face so that audiences would not

Lester Young and Count Basie

Lester Young grew up in Woodville, Mississippi. As a boy, he toured the country with his family, who were carnival musicians. He went to New York as the replacement for Coleman Hawkins in Fletcher Henderson's orchestra. That engagement did not work out well because none of the other band members liked Lester's sound. Lester left the group and hooked up with Count Basie's orchestra in 1936.

Count Basie learned to play piano from his mother as a boy. As a young man, he was involved in the Harlem music scene and studied informally with Fats Waller. Fats Waller was a prominent jazz composer and pianist, famous for songs he wrote, such as "Valentine Stomp," as well as for his

Lester Young and Count Basie
(continued)

performances on some of the greatest jazz tunes of all time, such as his organ playing on "St. Louis Blues." Before Count Basie was twenty years old, he toured all over America on the vaudeville circuit. Vaudeville is a kind of live variety show that is a blend of comedy sketches, singing, and dancing. Many musicians earned their living playing for vaudeville shows or for the silent movies. Count Basie played for both vaudeville and the silent movies.

Lester Young, Billie Holiday's friend, was a part of Count Basie's orchestra during the 1930s. By the end of the decade, the orchestra had achieved international fame. Billie Holiday sang with the orchestra regularly in 1937. She toured with Count Basie directly after she learned of her father's death.

get upset and think she was a white woman singing with a black band. Billie refused. Her next engagement with a band would be when she sang with Artie Shaw's orchestra.

The End of the 1930s

Billie Holiday sang with Artie Shaw's orchestra in 1938. Artie was considered a rival of Benny Goodman's, and he was becoming more and more famous. Billie's stint in Shaw's orchestra marked one of the first times that a black woman had sung with a white band. It was a moment of great significance in history and in music history, but unfortunately the association did not last long.

The trouble began when the band was touring, trying to make a name for themselves so they could perform in big hotels and concert halls in New York City. All over the South, Billie Holiday had trouble being served in restaurants. She had problems finding hotels that would admit blacks. She dreaded getting sick because it was so difficult to find a doctor who would give her the proper treatment.

Billie Holiday sings, accompanied by *(left to right)* bassist Johnny Williams, trumpeter Frankie Newton, and saxophonists Stan Payne and Kenneth Hollon, during a recording session for Commodore Records.

It is uncertain exactly why Billie Holiday left Artie's orchestra. Holiday maintained that it was Artie's managers, not Artie himself, who were difficult to work with. She said they made her sit by herself in dark rooms, waiting for her turn onstage. She was not permitted to sit in the audience at white clubs because of segregation. Billie also said that her time onstage kept getting whittled down. When the band was well known enough to play big clubs and hotels in New York City, Billie Holiday didn't get to share in the band's success because of her color. Hotel owners would make her enter the hotels through the back doors and the freight elevators instead of coming in with the rest of the band. Some even refused to include her singing when the band's performance at the hotel was broadcast nationally on the radio.

Billie left Artie's orchestra in 1939. She took her considerable talents downtown, to Greenwich Village and Cafe Society. She worked at Cafe Society for two years. It was at this club that she became a star. She worked seven nights a

week, for $75 a week. It was at this time that Billie recorded "Strange Fruit" for Commodore Records, because Columbia Records refused to record the song. In fact, after 1939, John Hammond never recorded Billie Holiday again. "Strange Fruit" is the song that put Billie Holiday on the map.

4

Celebrated and Disgraced

"Strange Fruit" helped to make Billie Holiday a celebrity. It also changed the way the public viewed her singing. Billie was extremely creative in the way she re-created a song. Singing "Strange Fruit" helped prove that she was a great actress, also. She became known for her dramatic

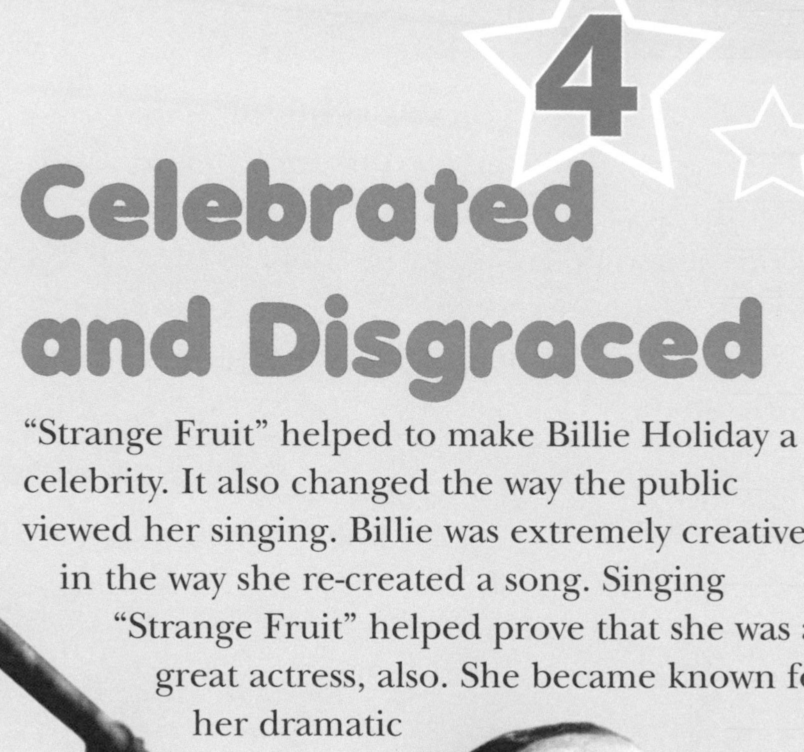

performance of songs. John Hammond thought that the song killed her creativity and locked her into having to do dramatic material. Not everyone agreed with him, though, because Billie still had plenty of fans.

Working Girl

After Cafe Society made Billie Holiday a star, she worked on 52nd Street between Fifth and Sixth Avenues. This was called "the Street" or "Swing Street" because there were so many jazz clubs there. Billie was Swing Street's highest-paid performer at that time. She earned about $1,000 a week. People flocked to see her performing the melancholy songs that seemed to give a voice to how sad everyone was feeling because of the influence of World War II.

Billie made two of her most famous records, "God Bless the Child" and "Gloomy Sunday," in 1941. As the story goes, Billie got the idea for "God Bless the Child" when she asked her mother for some money and her mother refused to give it to her. Sadie Fagan had always wanted to run a restaurant, and Billie had given her mother much of the money to start the short-lived Mom Holiday's restaurant. So when her mother denied her the money, Billie got angry and said, "God bless the child that's got his own," then wrote the lyrics to the song shortly afterward. Billie's career wasn't the only thing that was sizzling at this time. At twenty-four years old, her love life was heating up. She was about to get married.

Fun Fact!

Billie Holiday was known for having dogs, mostly little breeds such as Chihuahuas. She brought her dogs with her when she performed at clubs. She fed them using a baby's bottle. Her dogs, much like the white gardenias she loved, became one of her trademarks.

Jimmy Monroe and Heroin

Jimmy Monroe was the younger brother of Clarke Monroe, who ran the

Billie Holiday, an avid dog lover, at home listening to records in 1945.

Uptown House in Harlem, a club Billie had sung in frequently. Although she was performing on Swing Street, she still went uptown to hear her friends play music, and that's where she met Jimmy Monroe. He was handsome and charming. He and Billie eloped in 1941. Her mother and her friends thought Jimmy wasn't good for Billie, but that only made him more attractive to the headstrong woman.

Some say Jimmy was the one who gave Billie heroin for the first time. Still others say she started using the drug after she and Jimmy broke up, or that it was her second husband, Joe Guy, who first gave it to her. Jimmy did use heroin himself, though. Billie described in her autobiography how she felt like she was a slave to the drug. She made a lot of money, but she was not free. She had a habit that controlled her. She admitted later, after she found herself with a habit she was unable to kick, "If you think you need stuff to play music or sing, you're crazy. It can fix you so you can't play nothing or sing nothing."

Billie and Jimmy's marriage began to fall apart after about a year. Billie went to California to sing in some clubs, and Jimmy went with her. After the club she'd been working in shut down abruptly, leaving Billie without a source of income, she decided to go back to New York. However, Jimmy decided to stay in Los Angeles.

Decca Records

In 1941, Billie had some great recording dates with Decca, during which she recorded some songs she named among her favorites, such as "Fine and Mellow," and songs that became a standard part of her act, such as "Don't Explain." Billie wrote the song after her husband, Jimmy Monroe, came home one night with another woman's lipstick on his collar.

Holiday's career was still going well in the mid-1940s. In 1943, she had been voted best vocalist in a jazz critics poll sponsored by *Esquire* magazine. In 1944, she signed an official contract with Decca Records. Her friend Milt Gabler, who had wanted her to record "Strange Fruit," worked at Decca. It was at this record company that she began to record with strings, which

Billie Holiday sings at a recording session for Decca Records, the company she signed with in 1945.

she was only too happy to do. It was difficult in those days to get session musicians who played string instruments, and only the top stars got to record with strings. You can hear a great example of how wonderful Billie sounds with string accompaniment on tunes like "Lover Man," which was recorded at this time.

The Beginning of Billie's Decline

Billie sang at New York City's Town Hall in 1945. It was her first performance in a concert hall, and John Hammond called it "a triumph." She did not know at the time how familiar concert hall singing would become to her. Billie also toured for much of 1945 with a band led by her then lover, Joe Guy, whom she later married.

When the tour was over, Billie went back to New York City to play a long engagement at the Downbeat Club. But there was very bad news waiting for Billie. Sadie Fagan, Billie's mother, had passed away. Sadie had been the one person who Billie could love and trust completely.

When she died, she left her daughter feeling completely alone in what often seemed to her a hostile, difficult world. Sadie's death seemed to be the start of a downward spiral for Billie.

Under the inescapable influence of World War II, much of the world was changing. That included the music world in New York City. Club owners started to abandon Swing Street in favor of Broadway, where they could make more money. Holiday earned $1,000 a week on Broadway, but most of it went for the heroin she could no longer do without. Joe Guy was a heroin addict, and Billie's heroin use increased as a result. She was making plenty of money, but a lot of it was spent on drugs. Billie had been smoking marijuana for years, and back then they did not know that marijuana often paves the way for debilitating addiction—a sad fact that contributed heavily to Billie's decline in later years.

New Orleans and Heroin

In 1946, Decca Records signed Billie to another two-year contract. She worked most of this year at the Downbeat Club, but she took time off to go to Hollywood, California, with Louis Armstrong to make the feature film *New Orleans*, in which she played the role of a maid. She was disgusted with having to play a maid. In fact, she tried to get her manager to get her out of the contract, but he couldn't. She made the film, which got poor reviews. Louis Armstrong had been her idol from when she was a little girl, and she could console herself for having had to play a maid with the thought that she'd had a chance to work with him.

It was around this time that Holiday's heroin addiction seemed to be getting so out of control that it affected her career. She had always been a thorough professional, but now club owners had to watch her carefully. She began to show up late for performances. Sometimes she missed performances altogether, something she never would have done before. Holiday began wearing elbow-length gloves to cover the marks on her arms from injecting heroin. This was a signal to many of her friends and coworkers that Billie had a serious drug problem.

Billie Holiday sings on the set of *New Orleans*, in which she acted with Louis Armstrong.

At this time, Holiday had some difficult choices to make. Her heroin addiction was affecting her career. However, she was so addicted to the drug that she became sick with withdrawal symptoms when she didn't take it. It is a well-known fact that the symptoms of heroin withdrawal are so painful and debilitating that they make it even harder for a drug user to stop using.

In 1947, Billie decided to seek help for her drug addiction. She was hospitalized at a sanatorium in New York. She spent three weeks getting clean, under the supervision of trained medical staff. She had been promised complete privacy by the staff at the sanatorium, but rumors of her addiction leaked to the public and to the United States Bureau of Narcotics. When she returned to her career, federal narcotics agents trailed her wherever she went, hoping to catch her using drugs again. She was treated like a criminal. All of the familiar pressures of her life got her back to using heroin.

In May 1947, Billie was arrested for possession of narcotics. Federal agents from the Bureau of

Narcotics raided her hotel room as she performed at the Earle Theater in Philadelphia, Pennsylvania. Billie found out that agents were searching her room. She jumped into a car and drove quickly back to New York City. The federal agents found her a few days later and arrested her. She signed away her right to a lawyer. Joe Guy, who was arrested along with her, went free on technicalities. Neither her lawyer nor her agent would help her. She was sick from being without heroin. In court, she testified that she was spending $500 a week on heroin. Holiday had been told that if she pleaded guilty, she would be given a hospital cure to get her off of heroin. Instead, she was convicted as a criminal and sent to the Federal Women's Reformatory at Alderson, West Virginia, for a year and a day.

Billie's Experience at Alderson

Holiday's experience at Alderson was horrible. She went through heroin withdrawal cold turkey, a process that is painful and that can be fatal because it leaves a person's body in a weakened condition. In addition to having to come off heroin so abruptly, she was given menial labor to do. She was not shown any of the letters and gifts that were sent to her by her many fans all over the world. Holiday never once sang during the time she was in jail. When asked to sing, her answer was that she was there to be punished, and that was that. She spent nine and a half months in prison before being released early for good behavior.

On March 16, 1948, Billie was released from prison. She was thirty pounds heavier, but she was actually a lot healthier than she had been when she was arrested. Billie took a train to Newark, New Jersey. Fellow musician and friend Bobby Tucker met her at the station. He drove her to his mother's farm near Morristown, New Jersey, where she could relax.

She had not sung during her time at Alderson, and she was worried that her voice might have changed. The first thing she and Bobby did at the farm was to sing "Night and Day," which is a very hard song to sing. But despite the difficulty of the song, Billie hit the notes.

Billie was excited about getting back to singing professionally. She was soon to find out how difficult maintaining her career would become. The arrest and the time spent in prison had affected her working life in ways that she was just about to discover.

5

The Late 1940s and Early 1950s

Holiday's arrest led to her losing her cabaret license. This was a serious setback in her career. Being without a cabaret license meant that she could not perform in nightclubs or any place where liquor was sold more than four days at a time. This meant that none of her old friends could hire her. She did a successful concert at Carnegie Hall in 1948, just eleven days after her release from prison. She also did a Broadway engagement that lasted for three weeks.

Getting Back on Track

Holiday then began singing illegally in the Ebony Club, which later would become Birdland, a famous New York City jazz club. Holiday's lover at the time, John Levy, ran the club. When the Ebony Club closed during the summer, Billie sang at the Strand Theater on Broadway with Count Basie's orchestra. Thousands of fans came to hear her sing with the legendary Basie. Billie was somewhat bitter about it, thinking that many came to see her because they had heard she was using drugs. She claimed the audience came to see whether she was stoned or whether she really could still sing as well as ever. "The only reason they're out there is to see me fall into the damn orchestra pit," she said.

In time, John Levy came to have total control over Billie. John kept the $3,500 a week that Billie earned at the Strand Theater on Broadway. He controlled all of her finances and doled out money as if he was supporting her, instead of the other way around. He kept her in Cadillacs and minks, but there are many who say he was abusive to her.

Holiday spent most of the beginning of 1949 on the West Coast. In January, when John and Billie were in San Francisco, California, John tried to frame Holiday on a narcotics charge. She was able to convince the judge that the drugs were not hers, thanks to a lot of time, money, and a good lawyer. But Billie still had to stand trial because federal narcotics agents had found drugs in the hotel room she shared with John. She underwent a series of drug tests to prove that she was clean. On her return to New York City in the summer, Billie did a concert at the Apollo Theater. Shortly after, she recorded some songs at Decca Records. Lester Young was backing her up on the first recording session. However, she was soon to lose her friend Milt Gabler as her A&R manager when Decca assigned him to work for another of their recording studios, Coral.

The Early 1950s

The negative publicity was crucifying Billie's career. She referred to herself as a "DP," or a displaced person, which is what refugees were called after World War II. And with her career difficulties came a return to using heroin. The 1950s are regarded by many as the period of Billie Holiday's decline. However, she still continued to record and perform during these years. She was making plans for records and concerts even on her deathbed. That was the spirit of Billie Holiday. Music was a part of her. It was certainly the most valuable and enjoyable part of her life.

She signed a recording contract with Norman Granz in 1952. Norman was a jazz promoter and producer who would later become jazz legend Ella Fitzgerald's manager. The recordings that Billie did with Norman would eventually be released under the Verve label. She rerecorded a lot of her old hits, such as "God Bless the Child" and "Strange Fruit." Billie worked with Norman for five years.

Lady Day in 1950, at the beginning of the decade that many say yielded her finest work

Billie made sure that the recording sessions were not overarranged. As could be seen from the early days of her career, especially in her enjoyment of working with Count Basie's orchestra, Billie loved to improvise. Norman tried to give these sessions a more improvised, relaxed feeling. This was very much unlike the Decca recordings, which had been more arranged.

The toll that her drug use had taken on her voice is clear from these later recordings. Her voice is raspy in a way that it never had been before. Many people believe that Billie's work in the 1950s is a pitiful shadow of her earlier work. However, there are just as many people who disagree. Fans of the 1950s Billie Holiday recordings say that her voice had an almost telepathic ability to get right into your soul and express what you were feeling as you were listening. Fans say that her considerable dramatic techniques—her ability to communicate the lyrics of a song—were at their finest during the 1950s. Among the fans of her later work is jazz great Miles Davis, who said

Well into the 1950s, Lady Day kept performing live in front of American and European audiences.

her later work was "more mature." Her many fans tuned in to see Billie's comeback television special that aired in 1953. Artie Shaw was part of the group of musicians who accompanied her during the special. "I'm always making a comeback but nobody ever tells me where I've been," joked Billie.

The Royal Albert Hall and the Newport Festival

In 1954, Billie Holiday went on her first European tour. She had always dreamed of performing in Europe, and now she was getting the chance to do just that. She had had many European fans even in the early days of her career, and Billie had a great time touring Europe. The tour lasted for three weeks. She sang to audiences in Scandinavia, Germany, Holland, Belgium, France, Switzerland, and England. In England, she sang in London at the Royal Albert Hall. There were 6,000 people in the appreciative crowd! Billie referred to that concert as "the biggest thrill of my life." She felt appreciated in Europe in a way she had never felt in the United States.

That same year, back in the United States, *Down Beat* magazine gave her a special award, calling her "one of the all-time great vocalists in jazz." She also performed that year in the first Newport Jazz Festival. The festival is still held every year in Newport, Rhode Island. Her dear friend Lester Young was one of the musicians who played with her, even though he had not been feeling too well. Teddy Wilson, who had played with her on some of her earliest recordings, also played with her at the Newport Jazz Festival.

Louis McKay and Another Arrest

In 1956, Billie married Louis McKay. He went with her on an extended tour of the United States and Europe. Some people believe that he gave Billie a sense of security. Others say that he was a brutal man who was terribly abusive. Memry Midgett, who played piano for Billie

A worn-out Billie Holiday leaves a Philadelphia police station with her dog after her arrest on narcotics charges in February 1956.

in the 1950s, said, "[He was] one of the most ruthless men I have ever met. He exploited Billie Holiday completely."

The couple were arrested in February 1956. Billie was charged with possession of narcotics, and Louis was arrested for illegally possessing a gun. Billie returned to New York City when she was released on bail and entered a drug clinic. At the clinic, doctors helped her to go off heroin gradually, unlike how she had gone off it before. She was prescribed drugs that made the withdrawal process easier to bear. In fact, the treatment was successful initially. Some say Billie did not go back to using heroin at all. Some say that she was able to stay clean for longer periods of time but that she did go back to using heroin eventually. What is certain is that she started to drink alcohol. She drank as much as two bottles of liquor a day.

Lady Sings the Blues

Also in 1956, Billie told the details of her life to her friend William Dufty, who was a journalist at the *New York Post*. Billie wanted William to ghostwrite her autobiography. A ghostwriter is a person who writes a book for someone else to take credit for authoring the book. The book was published in 1956 as *Lady Sings the Blues.* The title is ironic given the fact that Billie had never wanted to be classified as a blues singer. She always insisted that, if the music critics had to have a label for her at all, she should be called a jazz singer.

Billie had glossed over certain facts of her life, such as the fact that her mother and father were never married. But she did describe in detail the unpleasant aspects of her life, such as her childhood traumas and drug addiction. There are plenty of passages in the book that read as cautionary tales for those who think drugs are glamorous. Billie gave plenty of advice in the book about the dangers of drug addiction.

The book got mixed reviews. Many who knew her personally were upset by the version of events reflected in the book, knowing them not to be absolutely truthful. Her friend, musician Leonard Feather, said it was "such a bizarre blend of fact, wishful thinking, rationalization, distortion and falsification that it is extremely hard, even for one who has known her, to determine where truth ends and fiction begins."

Billie gave two concerts at Carnegie Hall in New York City to promote her book. During both of them, someone read parts of *Lady Sings the Blues* aloud. Then Billie sang in between the spoken excerpts of the book. Fans got to see an

Fun Fact!

Did you know that a movie was made of *Lady Sings the Blues*? It was released in 1972, and it starred Diana Ross as Billie Holiday and Billy Dee Williams as the handsome Louis McKay. The real Louis McKay said of the movie, "I really like the way it shows the relationship she and I had. Billie and I were very much in love, although we had our problems."

intimate portrait of a woman who had been called one of the greatest jazz singers ever.

The Late 1950s

Despite a *Down Beat* article in which Billie had told a reporter, "I just want to be a housewife and take care of Mr. McKay," Billie and Louis McKay separated in 1957, when she was forty-two years old. She filed for a divorce, but the decree never became final. Once again by herself, Holiday began to hole up in her apartment, drinking, smoking, and watching television. The only thing she had for comfort was her dog. Billie was famous for her cute little dogs, mostly Chihuahuas. She often brought them with her to Cafe Society and other clubs where she sang every night.

The excessive use of alcohol eventually took a toll on her career, as well as on her private life. Billie showed up drunk for recording sessions and even for performances. During some of her performances, people had to help her get to the microphone. Still, there were

Billie with professional dancer Bill Robinson at New York City's Ebony Club in May 1948

exceptional moments in what had been a long and glorious career. Billie sang "Fine and Mellow" in late 1957 on *The Sound of Jazz* television broadcast on CBS. She was joined by Lester Young and other musicians who had played with her in the past. By all accounts, it was an extremely emotional and moving performance.

Billie recorded in 1958, although she showed up for the sessions with a bottle of gin that she would proceed to finish during the sessions. Holiday's 1958 album, *Lady in Satin*, took months to record, but it became one of her best-selling albums. Also during this time, Billie took two trips to Europe to perform. But even her appreciative fan base in Europe noticed the change in Lady Day. Still, she felt so comfortable in Europe that she talked about moving to England, but she never got close to even planning such a thing.

In 1959, Billie attended the funeral of her friend Lester Young. She arrived with a bottle of gin stashed in her purse. She wanted to sing at his funeral, but his wife told her that she couldn't. Young's wife said later that Billie looked very upset and unstable, and she had been worried that Billie would make a scene. "I'll be the next one to go," Billie told friends at Young's funeral.

Billie celebrated her forty-fourth birthday on April 7, 1959, just a few weeks after Lester Young's death. The friends who were at her apartment were struck by how pretty and healthy she looked. There was an enormous amount of food there, which Billie had cooked herself, such as chicken and black-eyed peas, and which was reminiscent of the days that Sadie Fagan had been alive. However, this bloom of apparent health would not last for long.

6

The End, the Legacy

Billie Holiday continued to perform through April 1959. She did several concerts in Boston, Massachusetts. But one month later, at the Phoenix Theater in Greenwich Village, Holiday had to be helped off the stage during the show. She had been able to complete only two songs. She collapsed as soon as she was out of sight of the audience. It was her last public appearance.

Billie's Collapse

Billie's friend Leonard Feather followed her into her dressing room to make sure that she was OK. He searched her face, visibly concerned for her. She stared at him, in a daze. "What's the matter, Leonard?" she asked him. "You seen a ghost or something?"

After the show at the Phoenix Theater, several of her friends, including Leonard Feather and her agent Joe Glaser, tried to convince Billie to check into a hospital, but she refused. Some say that she had a fear of hospitals because she could not easily get drugs when she was in there. She told her friends not to worry. She said she had people around her who were helping to take care of her. She said she was practicing for a concert in Toronto that would take place the following Monday and that she would be able to perform.

Holiday collapsed again on May 31, 1959, in her apartment. The jazz singer Frankie Freedom was the one who found her unconscious on the floor of her apartment. He called an ambulance,

By the end of the 1950s, Billie's health had started to deteriorate after the years of abuse she had put her body through.

even though Billie had always told him not to call one if she got sick because she didn't want to go to the hospital. Freedom called one anyway, saying that "Mrs. Eleanora McKay" was extremely ill and needed to go to the hospital immediately.

Of course no one knew who Mrs. Eleanora McKay was, so Holiday got no special treatment

when she arrived at the hospital. They looked at the numerous track marks on her arms and concluded that she was just another poor junkie. Her private doctor was called, and she was transferred to a ward in Metropolitan Hospital. As her friends started to pull some strings and lay down some money, Billie got a private room. At first none of her friends could get in to see her. The hospital policy was that only family members could visit with her. So her friends had to get crafty. They called some of her family members.

They called Kay Kelly,

Did You Know?

The United States Postal Service created a commemorative stamp of Billie Holiday. The stamp, issued on September 17, 1994, depicts her wearing her trademark white gardenia in her hair. There is also a French phone card dedicated to Billie Holiday.

who was the daughter of Phil Gough, Sadie's husband. Kelly was not terribly close to Billie, and she was not a blood relative, but she got in to see her. William Dufty also got in to see her because he flashed his press pass. Joe Glaser called Louis McKay, who was still Billie's legal husband. Louis flew in from California. Even though Louis and Billie were separated, Joe Glaser thought that Louis might make himself useful around the hospital. He could be used to run errands or get things in to Billie when none of her friends could get in to see her.

William Dufty said of seeing her in the hospital, "She was weak, but she was completely conscious. She was never one to waste words, anyway; the grip and the economy were still there and she said something that day about a comeback. 'They'll call this a comeback.' She didn't seem like someone who was dying."

Lady at the Met

Billie told William that she needed some money, and so he arranged for her to get a series of articles published about what she was going through in the hospital. They were published in *Confidential* magazine. Billie loved to read this magazine; she had plenty of issues of it in her hospital room. William wrote a racy, tell-all piece called "How Heroin Saved My Life." The magazine changed the title to "I Needed Heroin to Live." Billie received $840 for the article. She gave $90 to William as a payment for his writing the article.

Meanwhile, Louis McKay showed up at Metropolitan Hospital with a contract. He wanted Billie to sign it, turning over to him the rights to *Lady Sings the Blues.* But he also needed William Dufty's signature, and there was no way that William was going to sign such a contract. However, William did not want to get Louis angry because he could still be useful around the hospital. Together they managed to delay the matter.

Billie talked with her friends about doing a concert from the Metropolitan Hospital. One of her friends told her she should call it Lady at the Met. Holiday loved the idea and was happy thinking about planning the concert. Then a nurse found a packet of heroin in Holiday's room. The nurse claimed that she could see dots of the white powder around Holiday's nose. Holiday actively denied sniffing heroin. Her friends rushed to her defense, saying that she was on methadone and was not using heroin anymore. Someone may have left it in the room as a "favor" or as an attempt to get Billie in trouble.

All the same, Billie was arrested in her hospital bed for possession of narcotics. The arrest meant that all of her luxuries were taken away from her. She was not allowed to have a radio, a record player, or her magazines. Billie was miserable. She was in an oxygen tent almost all the time now. Eventually, she sank into a coma. She had been in the hospital for forty-four days when a chaplain came to give her the last rites. Billie was a Catholic, as Sadie Fagan had been.

One hour before Holiday's death, a nurse gave William the $750 she had found on Billie Holiday's body when she had been attending her. It was the money Holiday had saved from the *Confidential* piece. She told the nurse she wanted

"Bill" to have it. But William did not accept the money. He asked the nurse to put it with Billie's personal property. It was all the money she had in the world. There was only seventy cents in her bank account.

Thousands of mourners came to pay respects at Billie Holiday's funeral.

Holiday died on June 17, 1959, "of various heart, kidney, and liver ailments that were fatally complicated by a lung blockage." William Dufty had wanted her funeral to be at St. Patrick's Cathedral in New York City, but that was not possible. It was held at St. Paul the Apostle Cathedral on 60th Street and Ninth Avenue. Three thousand people came to the funeral service. There had been a wake the day before. Billie had been laid out in her favorite pink lace gown and gloves.

Pallbearers carry Billie Holiday into St. Paul the Apostle Cathedral in New York City in June 1959.

Frank Sinatra is one of the many vocal legends who was greatly inspired by Billie Holiday's singing.

Billie Holiday's Legacy

Frank Sinatra described Billie Holiday as the single greatest influence on his singing. There are many artists who feel the same way about her. After Billie Holiday's performances and recordings, music was changed forever. Her influence can still be seen today in such singers as Macy Gray. Macy Gray has been billed as this generation's Billie Holiday for her soulful way of singing.

Billie was inducted into the Rock and Roll Hall of Fame in 2000. She was inducted into the Early Influences category for her legendary work in blues and jazz. This recognition for her

incredible talent was surely well-deserved.

Leonard Feather said of her: "Billie Holiday's voice was the voice of living intensity of soul in the true sense of that greatly abused word. As a human being she was sweet, sour, kind, mean, generous, profane, lovable and impossible, and nobody who knew her expects to see anyone quite like her again." The words of her friend perfectly illustrate the complex person that Billie Holiday was. She was a great musician with an enormous musical talent. She was a passionate woman who had been unlucky in love. She was a friend to many. She was a loving, if headstrong, daughter. Billie Holiday had many roles to play in her lifetime.

Contemporary artists like Macy Gray also credit Holiday as an inspiration.

SELECTED DISCOGRAPHY

1942 *Billie's Blues*
1946 *New Orleans*
1952 *Solitude: Billie Holiday Story Vol. 2*
1954 *Recital By: The Billie Holiday Story Vol. 3*
1955 *Music for Torching: Billie Holiday Story Vol. 5*
1956 *Lady Sings the Blues*
1956 *At Carnegie Hall: The Billie Holiday Story Vol. 6*
1957 *Body and Soul*
1957 *Songs for Distingue Lovers*
1958 *At Monterey/1958*
1958 *Lady in Satin*
1959 *Last Recording*

GLOSSARY

A&R Artist and repertoire; people responsible for discovering new talent.

autobiography A book written by someone about his or her own life story.

brothel A house of prostitution.

debilitating Characterized by having the ability to make weak or to take strength away.

ghostwriter A writer who allows someone else to take credit for his or her writing.

improvisation Making music up as you go along instead of working from sheet music.

ironic Something that is marked with incongruity or that ends up different from what was expected.

menial Something that is unimportant or considered lowly.

Prohibition A period of United States history when it was illegal to buy, sell, drink, or make alcohol.

reformatory A house of correction.

refugee A person who flees to escape danger or persecution.

repertoire Songs that an artist knows how to perform and that he or she performs regularly.

sanatorium A hospital for the care of the chronically ill.

segregation The policy of forcing blacks and whites to live as separately as possible.

speakeasy A place where illegal alcohol was sold during Prohibition.

TO FIND OUT MORE

The Billie Holiday Theatre
1368 Fulton Street
Brooklyn, NY 11216
(718) 636-0918
Web site: http://www.thebillieholiday.org

Rock and Roll Hall of Fame and Museum
One Key Plaza
Cleveland, OH 44114
(888) 764-ROCK (7625)
Web site: http://www.rockhall.com

Rock and Roll Hall of Fame Foundation
1290 Avenue of the Americas
New York, NY 10104

Web Sites

Due to the changing nature of Internet links, the Rosen Publishing Group, Inc., has developed an online list of Web sites related to the subject of this book. This site is updated regularly. Please use this link to access the list:

http://www.rosenlinks.com/rrhf/bhol/

FOR FURTHER READING

Chilton, John. *Billie's Blues: The Billie Holiday Story, 1933–1959.* New York: Da Capo Press, 1989.

Clarke, Donald. *Wishing on the Moon: The Life & Times of Billie Holiday.* New York: Viking Penguin, 1995.

Davis, Angela Y. *Blues Legacies and Black Feminism: Gertrude "Ma" Rainey, Bessie Smith, and Billie Holiday.* New York: Pantheon Books, 1998.

Gourse, Leslie. *Billie Holiday: The Tragedy and Triumph of Lady Day.* Danbury, CT: Franklin Watts, Inc., 1995.

Margolick, David. *Strange Fruit: Billie Holiday, Cafe Society, and an Early Cry for Civil Rights.* Philadelphia, PA: Running Press Book Publishers, 2000.

Works Cited

Holiday, Billie, with William Dufty. *Lady Sings the Blues.* New York: Viking Penguin, 1984.

Kliment, Bud. *Billie Holiday.* Broomall, PA: Chelsea House Publishers, 1990.

O'Meally, Robert. *Lady Day: The Many Faces of Billie Holiday.* New York: Arcade Publishing, Inc., 1993.

INDEX

A

American Record Corporation (ARC), 45, 47
Apollo Theater, 10, 43–45, 74
Armstrong, Louis, 6, 19, 20, 40–41, 42, 65

B

Basie, Count, 35, 37, 41, 47, 48 49–50, 73, 77
Beiderbecke, Bix, 42
Billy Holiday Theatre, 33

C

Cafe Society, 10, 54–55, 57, 86
Carnegie Hall, 10, 72, 85
Coltrane, John, 35
Columbia Records, 32, 42, 55
Commodore Records, 55
Cooper, Frank, 43

D

Davis, Miles, 77–80
Dean, Alice, 19, 22
Decca Records, 61–63, 64, 74, 77
"Don't Explain," 61
Downbeat Club, 63, 65
DuBois, W. E. B., 27
Dufty, William, 12, 83, 94–95, 96–97

E

Ebony Club (Birdland), 73
Ellington, Duke, 41

F

Fagan, Sadie (mother), 16, 18, 19, 22–23, 28, 29–30, 60, 96
- Billie's birth and, 13–14
- death of, 63–64
- illness and, 30, 31
- as maid, 15
- marriage to Phil Gough, 20
- restaurant of, 33–35, 57–58, 89

Feather, Leonard, 84–85, 91, 101
Federal Women's Reformatory, Alderson, WV, 69–70
"Fine and Mellow," 61, 88
Fitzgerald, Ella, 19, 75
Freedom, Frankie, 91–92

G

Gabler, Milt, 61, 74
Glaser, Joe, 45, 46, 91, 94
"Gloomy Sunday," 57
"God Bless the Child," 8–10, 57–58, 75
Goodman, Benny, 8, 36, 37, 41–43, 51
Gough, Phil, 20, 94

Granz, Norman, 75–77
Gray, Macy, 100
Great Depression, 6, 30
Guy, Joe (second husband), 60, 63, 64, 69

H

Hammond, John, 10–11, 14–15, 32, 36, 42, 45, 47, 55, 57, 63
Harlem, 10, 23, 26, 28, 30, 41, 49, 60
Harlem Renaissance, 26–27
Henderson, Fletcher, 14, 35, 45, 46, 49
Holiday, Billie
 with Artie Shaw, 51–54
 childhood of, 6, 13–23, 28–37
 with Columbia Records, 32, 55
 with Count Basie, 47–51, 73
 death of, 96–97
 with Decca Records, 61–63, 64, 74, 77
 decline of, 63–64, 65–71, 72, 75, 77, 81–83, 86, 88–89, 90–91
 dogs and, 58, 86
 drug/alcohol addiction, 11, 18, 60, 64, 65–70, 73, 75, 77, 83, 84, 86, 88–89, 91–93, 96
 early interest in music, 19–20, 35
 early jobs held, 6, 19, 23
 in Europe, 80–81, 88
 fame and, 54–55, 56–57, 61, 81
 in Harlem, 10, 23, 28–37, 43
 influences of, 6, 20, 41
 last public appearance, 90
 legacy, 100–101
 marriages/romances, 42, 46, 58–60, 63, 73–74, 81–83, 85
 name change/real name, 13, 14
 in prison, 28–29, 69–70, 71, 72
 as prostitute, 23, 28
 racism and, 7–9, 45, 51, 54
 rape of, 22
 in reformatory, 22
 Rock and Roll Hall of Fame, induction into, 100–101
 start as singer, 30–32, 36–37
 style of singing, 6, 7, 19, 20, 56–57, 77
Holiday, Clarence (father), 6, 13–16, 30
 death of, 50

J

jazz, 40–41
 difference between blues and, 38–39

K

Kelly, Kay, 93–94

L

Lady in Satin, 11, 88
Lady Sings the Blues (autobiography), 12, 16–17, 84–85, 95

Levy, John, 73–74
"Lover Man," 63

M

McKay, Louis (third husband), 81–83, 85, 86, 94, 95
Monette's nightclub, 10, 32, 43
Monroe, Clarke, 58–60
Monroe, Jimmy (first husband), 46, 58–61
Morton, Jelly Roll, 39

N

New Orleans (movie), 65
Newport Jazz Festival, 81
"Night and Day," 70

P

Parker, Charlie, 6
Phoenix Theater, 90–91
Pod and Jerry's Log Cabin, 30, 31, 35, 47
Pollack, Ben, 42
Preston, Jerry, 30, 32
Prohibition, 10, 27, 45

R

racism, 7–9, 45, 51, 54
Rollins, Sonny, 35

S

segregation, 7, 54
Shaw, Artie, 8, 37, 51, 80
Sims, Sylvia, 46
Sinatra, Frank, 100
Smith, Bessie, 6, 18, 19, 20, 38
Sound of Jazz, The (television show), 88
speakeasies, 10, 16, 27–28
"St. Louis Blues," 18, 50
"Strange Fruit," 8, 55, 56, 61, 75
swing music/big band, 10, 14, 39, 41, 42
"Swing Street," 57, 60, 64

T

"Trav'lin All Alone," 31–32
Tucker, Bobby, 70

U

United States Bureau of Narcotics, 68–69
Uptown House, 46, 60

V

Verve Records, 75

W

Waller, Fats, 49–50
Wilson, Teddy, 42, 45, 47, 81

Y

Young, Lester, 6, 20, 35, 47, 49–50, 74, 81, 88
  death of, 88–89

About the Author

Magdalena Alagna is an editor and freelance writer living in New York City.

Photo Credits

Cover, pp. 4, 21, 29, 34, 36, 37, 40, 52–53, 59, 62, 76, 78–79, 92, 100 © Hulton/Archive/Getty Images; pp. 5, 9, 26, 44, 66–67, 82, 87, 90, 97, 98–99, 101 © Corbis; pp. 12, 56, 72 © AP/Wide World Photos.

Editor

Eliza Berkowitz

Series Design

Tom Forget

Layout

Nelson Sá